A TRUE & EXACT HISTORY:

a Reading

Published by Poinciana Paper Press
Nassau, The Bahamas

ISBN 978-0-9989150-1-2

Copyright © 2018 by Sonia Farmer

No part of this book can be reproduced in any form without permission in writing from the publisher

Book design by Sonia Farmer

All illustrations used throughout this book and on the cover are by Richard Ligon, *A True & Exact History of the Island of Barbadoes* (1657)

Cover texture image used under license from Shutterstock.com

A TRUE & EXACT
HISTORY

a
Reading

SONIA FARMER

POINCIANA PAPER PRESS

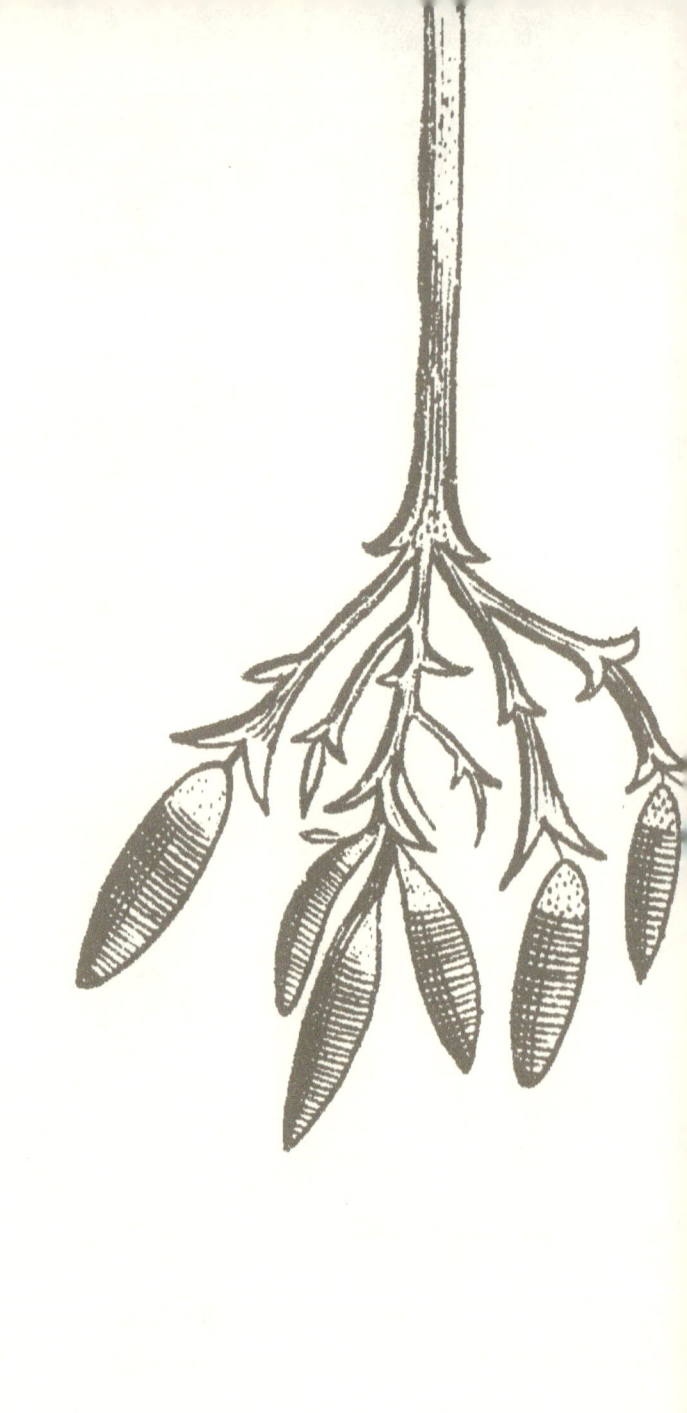

CAST:

SPEAKER ONE: *An ex-pat*

SPEAKER TWO: *An immigrant*

SPEAKER THREE: *An undocumented island resident*

SPEAKER FOUR: *An island citizen*

SPEAKER FIVE: *An African slave*

SPEAKER SIX: *An historian*

SPEAKER SEVEN: *A colonial slave master*

SPEAKER EIGHT: *An indigenous person of the Caribbean*

SPEAKER NINE: *The Edenic island*

SPEAKER TEN: *The colonized island*

SPEAKER ELEVEN: *The free nation*

mors sceptra ligonibus aequat

Palmeto Royall

The

ONE:
    I found myself a stranger
    in my own Countrey

    rather than abide here
    I continued to shift this ground

ONE & TWO:
    I have not felt rested
    in this Landscape

TWO:
    is there so narrow a room
    as I remember remaining in

    left so miserably burnt
    I could hardly
    discern colors

ONE & TWO:
    there is no land in
    a free heart
    mixt with Cruelties

TWO:
> I want the goodness of
> merciless enemies
>
> no other love is possible

ONE:
> Tyrants themselves
> follow this guide
> like a dear friend
>
> try fortune
> in another Element
>
> riseth to the top of the sea
> and begin a voyage

TWO:
> But to what Coast? There are none
> to prey on in ports of equal darkness

ONE & TWO:
> make fire

TWO:
> that light
> in the instant it is made
> hath the greater power
> to sharpen redeem'd
> out of wary Company

ONE:
> deliver upon them
> insufferable bodies
> scorching together

    the Cement of that
    made to hold
    a grave of language

ONE & TWO:
    such abuses
    we all were desirous for

TWO:
    when we land
    at the distance of speech
    we commit ourselves
    to have our throats cut

ONE:
    this body will hold
    silent
    amiss to express
    thick lipt beauties

ONE & TWO:
    I could not cast away
    the places I have named

TWO:
    they appeared as
    rare flowers that grow
    their necks
    as a badge of freedom

    open to speak
    in mute language
    to strangers
    in so publick a place

ONE:
>   I thought I had been sufficiently
>   armed with perfection
>
>   my heart
>   fixed fast in its
>   long kept habitation

ONE & TWO:
>   my love
>   could starve
>   in this posture

ONE:
>   leaving desire behind
>   in the midst of
>   smoak and fire
>
>   name a place
>   so totally deserted
>   it lay clouds doubtful
>   of latitude

TWO:
>   when we miss
>   the long reach of pleasure
>
>   the heavens
>   move that horizon
>   a further distance
>   from our wished Harbour

THREE:
    when our eyes
    grow to perfection
    secure shelter
    whilst they retribute their pains

FOUR:
    wanting witness
    we live
    in the distance
    of observation

THREE & FOUR:
    overlooking
    liberties of the past

THREE:
    our deadly hunger
    we carried
    from place to place

    plague the living
    and prove contagious

ONE, TWO, THREE & FOUR:
   I only speak
   in plain language
   as I hath been
   overgrown with
   beasts

FOUR:
   being here a prisoner
   is the greatest art
   that I am exactly made for

THREE:
   working
   to keep alive
   is a crime

FOUR:
   but easily led
   by the voices of sickness
   that live here

ONE—ELEVEN (*ascending in number & overlapping*):
   I suffer to remain

THREE & FOUR:
   Saint of a wild
   mad Land

THREE:
   I had an exact plot of memory
   desired in unwholesome thirst

FOUR:
>   our bodies
>   being exhausted with
>   our own Countreys
>   seldom drink
>
>   when they do
>   take your knife
>   eat deep into the steel

THREE:
>   no net can be compared
>   to this want we grow

FOUR:
>   yet spring
>   is not to be endured
>   without spoyl
>
>   these roots have a small
>   remainder of teeth

ONE, TWO, THREE & FOUR:
>   feed upon
>   the soil of this place

THREE:
>   larded with
>   the fat of the past
>   many burst
>   in pieces

FOUR:
>   home near the shoar
>   some had been bred
>   with freedom

THREE & FOUR:
>   and I found my power
>   to be serviceable to them

FOUR:
>   I dressed several wayes
>   and proved wanting

THREE:
>   come
>   open the heart
>   and lay in a dish

THREE & FOUR:
>   crack our teeth at the Table
>   where Land touch Sea

THREE:
>   for the honor of the Island

A Scale of :8:foote

FIVE:
> I could hardly stand upright
> when the heat of the day came
>
> I found the weakest rain within
> and left underground

ONE—FIVE:
> If I were to build myself
> in that place
> I would have a story

FIVE:
> and you shall feel the
> hot Country
> I grew weary of

SIX:
> to give you an exact account
> some gathered fire to wash themselves

SEVEN:
> tis a lovely sight to see
> men and women
> pilling off the skin of night

SIX:
> blood followed
> when they came home
>
> thin and
> unaccustomed to love
> being knockt out
> against a Cane

ONE—SEVEN:
> there is no way to stop
> the going on of this flame

FIVE:
> with naked feet
> I came away
>
> burnt
> his house
> down to the ground

SIX:
> this cruel revenge
> spread

FIVE, SIX & SEVEN:
> cut all the throats
> of courage

ONE—SEVEN:
> love has been
> a daring act

FIVE:
> our Gun-shots

    are fetch'd
    from several languages

    and by that means
    stark naked
    and most beautiful

SIX:
    every one of them
    beasts

    compelled to do
    as others do
    on their backs

FIVE, SIX & SEVEN:
    call'd home by
    the rope of pleasure
    in this hand

SEVEN:
    part them
    upon a hatchet
    of sharp desire
    learnt by heart

    the body could go
    without a head
    and may hold good

SIX:
    at a distance
    they remember
    their own Countrey

and want
the skill to hunt
letters and numbers

FIVE:
   they march with a pace
   meant to conquer their voices

   and therefore
   heard nothing
   of cruelties

SIX:
   secretly resolved
   to burn all others
   doubtful in this desire
   to know such languages
   as they had

SEVEN:
   any that live under the Sun
   have to set no great value
   upon their lives

FIVE, SIX & SEVEN:
   all these great casualties stand still
   in the mouth of the Furnace

FIVE:
   that red-hot devil
   have given them a horn
   to supply these losses
   from the River of heads

SIX:
> let us consider
> how to stop
> those mouths

FIVE, SIX & SEVEN:
> order
> whosoever nam'd the word
> or all those that heard him

ONE—SEVEN:
> Shot

SEVEN:
> good natur'd wild beasts
> never set foot
> upon this ground
>
> and if so
> they never liv'd

The Queens Pine.

EIGHT:
    I shall begin
    with the first name
    few know to carry

NINE:
    every man knows his own great want
    when they trespass upon her tune

    not for the sweetness
    but strangeness of it

EIGHT & NINE:
    I cannot
    speak their forms
    neither singing nor crying

EIGHT:
    all is husht
    forgotten amongst
    every part of
    our Garden

ONE—NINE:
    I come now
    to lose myself
    in a name

NINE:
    to be so firmly rooted in the earth
    you may remove
    those other places
    that can be imagined

EIGHT:
    I have nam'd
    the Roots I have set
    down already

NINE:
    and in a years time
    you will have
    the faculty of speech

EIGHT & NINE:
    to taste suddenly
    that body
    cast away

NINE:
    I have been told
    what shapes they bear
    out of your mouth

EIGHT:
    touch them
    till we cannot perceive

any island
that bears an English name

EIGHT & NINE:
any shape or colour
neither skin nor stone

ONE—NINE:
a most graceful diminution

NINE:
thin as
leaves of parchment

being opened by the Sun
long before
they were to suffer

EIGHT:
the form
is possible to discern

growing by degrees
an infinity of small roots

NINE:
if this earth were enough
it might be allowed to support
the weight of the first born

and not only the axes
that fell them

EIGHT & NINE:
never give over
the word

EIGHT:
>   hold it to the body
>   full of seeds
>   and plant new ones within

NINE:
>   a well shap't heart
>   continues opening
>
>   till it pulls
>   like a large fish-hook
>   a grove of fruit
>   not to be eaten

EIGHT & NINE:
>   I speak as a Crucifix

ONE—NINE:
>   professing the names
>   of his own cross

NINE:
>   come to perfection then
>   upon the edges of teeth
>
>   fall over one another
>   touching the ground

EIGHT:
>   fetch all the skin
>   off your mouth
>   before your tongue
>   have made an Eccho

EIGHT & NINE:
   full of an appetite
   beyond measure

A Scale of 8 feet.

TEN:
    a taste of the Iland
    brought thither
    a stranger

    who had the skill
    to know
    the sweetness
    it ought to have

ELEVEN:
    what manner of place
    is to be chosen
    upon the brow of fire

    If this husbandry
    burn the whole field
    secure the fire

ONE—ELEVEN:
    spirits should be brought
    having nothing

TEN:
> ready to be cast by
> one touch of this
> sweet Negotiation

TEN & ELEVEN:
> draw out
> your hand

TEN:
> you hold
> the form of a heart
> brought thither
> from other parts

ELEVEN:
> these seeds never bear
> rob'd of all earthly substance
>
> there remains nothing
> but that beat
> with a small store of Artillery

TEN & ELEVEN:
> forraign Forces
> lay their powder in
> and I came away

ONE—ELEVEN:
> divided into eleven

ELEVEN:
> a standing execution

TEN:
> every tree
> at the distance
> of stones cast

TEN & ELEVEN:
> falling

ONE—ELEVEN:
> no man knows
> this Island
> as much as we can

ELEVEN:
> all aches and bruises

TEN:
> take away
> this great beauty
> I love so violently

TEN & ELEVEN:
> and you shall feel that
> great love

ONE—ELEVEN:
> break necks

TEN:
> runaway

ELEVEN:
> I told you

ONE—ELEVEN:
    no Horizon can be seen

ELEVEN:
    the beauty of the
    Heavens
    are as far as Europe

TEN:
    we Mortals that love
    thrive between them

ONE—ELEVEN:
    not allowed in

TEN:
    you shall know
    by their shadows
    those Saints
    of middle earth

ELEVEN:
    every day
    more and more
    the pulse remains
    to account
    for our bargain

    your debts

TEN & ELEVEN:
    will grow ripe
    and impassable

ELEVEN, TEN & NINE:
   freedome is not
   a custom of the Island

ELEVEN, TEN, NINE & EIGHT:
   any man that saw me

ELEVEN—SEVEN:
   have slept within me

ELEVEN—SIX:
   such Organs

ELEVEN—FIVE:
   make amends

ELEVEN—FOUR:
   finding a home

ELEVEN—THREE:
   in the Harbor of
   my body

ELEVEN—TWO:
   being nothing

ELEVEN—ONE:
   but a strange Countrey

ELEVEN—ONE *(descending in number & overlapping)*:
   for ever and ever

ACKNOWLEDGEMENTS:

Written by Sonia Farmer, *A True and Exact History* is an erasure of Richard Ligon's *A True and Exact History of the Island of Barbadoes (1657)*. The resulting poem uses the language at the core of this text to interrogate narrative as a device of cohesive history in the Caribbean.

This project began in the Spring of 2016 during a writing residency when Annalee Davis pulled Ligon's text from the Colleen Lewis Reading Room at Fresh Milk in St. George, Barbados.

A limited-edition artist book was designed, printed, and boxed by Sonia Farmer at the University of Iowa in the Fall of 2017 and Spring of 2018 in an edition of 25 copies.

This artist book was first exhibited at The National Art Gallery of The Bahamas as part of the exhibition "We Suffer To Remain" which ran from March to July 2018, and to mark its finassage, the poem was reimagined as a sound piece. Using eleven speakers to represent the eleven separate parishes of the island, their voices inhabit and exchange threads of these dispersed narratives, ultimately calling into question what it means to write "a true and exact history" of anything.

The author wishes to thank the ten other readers who first performed this piece on July 29, 2018, in the ballroom of the National Art Gallery of The Bahamas: Mik Bancroft, Jason Evans, Yasmin Glinton, Jodi Minnis, Nicolette Bethel, Ian Bethell Bennett, Craig Smith, Patricia Glinton-Meicholas, Matthew Rahming, and Natalie Willis. Endless gratitude is also extended to Holly Bynoe and the entire team at the National Art Gallery of The Bahamas for providing the platform and encouragement to make this possible.

Sonia Farmer is a writer, visual artist, and small press publisher who uses letterpress printing, bookbinding, hand-papermaking, and digital projects to build narratives about the Caribbean space. She is the founder of Poinciana Paper Press, a small and independent press located in Nassau, The Bahamas, which produces handmade and limited edition chapbooks of Caribbean literature and promotes the crafts of book arts through workshops and creative collaborations. Her artwork has been exhibited throughout Nassau including at the National Art Gallery of The Bahamas. She is the author of *Infidelities* (Poinciana Paper Press, 2017) which was longlisted for the 2018 OCM Bocas Prize for Caribbean Literature. She has also self-published several chapbooks. Her poetry has won the 2011 Prize in the Small Axe Literary Competition and has appeared in various journals. She holds a BFA in Writing from Pratt Institute and is currently pursuing her MFA studies in Book Arts at the University of Iowa.

www.ingramcontent.com/pod-product-compliance
Lightning Source LLC
Chambersburg PA
CBHW030459010526
44118CB00011B/1016